P9-DVR-999

32175005293875

935   Odijk, Pamela,
Od   The Sumerians

DATE DUE

JUN 08 '9			
GAYLORD			PRINTED IN U.S.A.

The Sumerians

THE ANCIENT WORLD

The Sumerians

Pamela Odijk

Silver Burdett Press

Acknowledgments

The author and publishers are grateful to the following for permission to reproduce copyright photographs and prints:

ANT/M. F. Soper p. 13; Michael Holford pp. 9, 10–11, 14, 15, 26, 31, 34, 36–37, 38; Ron Sheridan's Photo-Library pp. 12, 16, 20, 21, 23, 25, 30, 32, 33, 35, 40.

While every care has been taken to trace and acknowledge copyright, the publishers tender their apologies for any accidental infringement where copyright has proven untraceable. They would be pleased to come to a suitable arrangement with the rightful owner in each case.

© Pamela Odijk 1989

All rights reserved. No part of this publication
may be reproduced or transmitted, in any
form or by any means, without permission.

First published 1989 by
THE MACMILLAN COMPANY OF AUSTRALIA PTY LTD
107 Moray Street, South Melbourne 3205
6 Clarke Street, Crows Nest 2065

Adapted and first published in the United States in 1990
by Silver Burdett Press, Englewood Cliffs, N.J.

Library of Congress Cataloging-in-Publication Data

Odijk, Pamela, 1942–
    The Sumerians / by Pamela Odijk.
        p.   cm.—(The Ancient world)
    "First published 1989 by the Macmillan Company of
Australia... adapted and first published in the United States in
1990"—T.p. verso.
    Summary: Describes the civilization of the Sumerians, who
inhabited the land which today is Iraq, in the beginning of the
fourth millennium B.C.
    1. Sumerians—Juvenile literature. [1. Sumerians.] I.
Title. II. Series: Odijk, Pamela, 1942–   Ancient world.
DS72.035   1990
935'.01—dc20   89-39570
    ISBN 0-382-09892-7   CIP
                                                    AC

The Sumerians

Contents

The Sumerians: Timeline

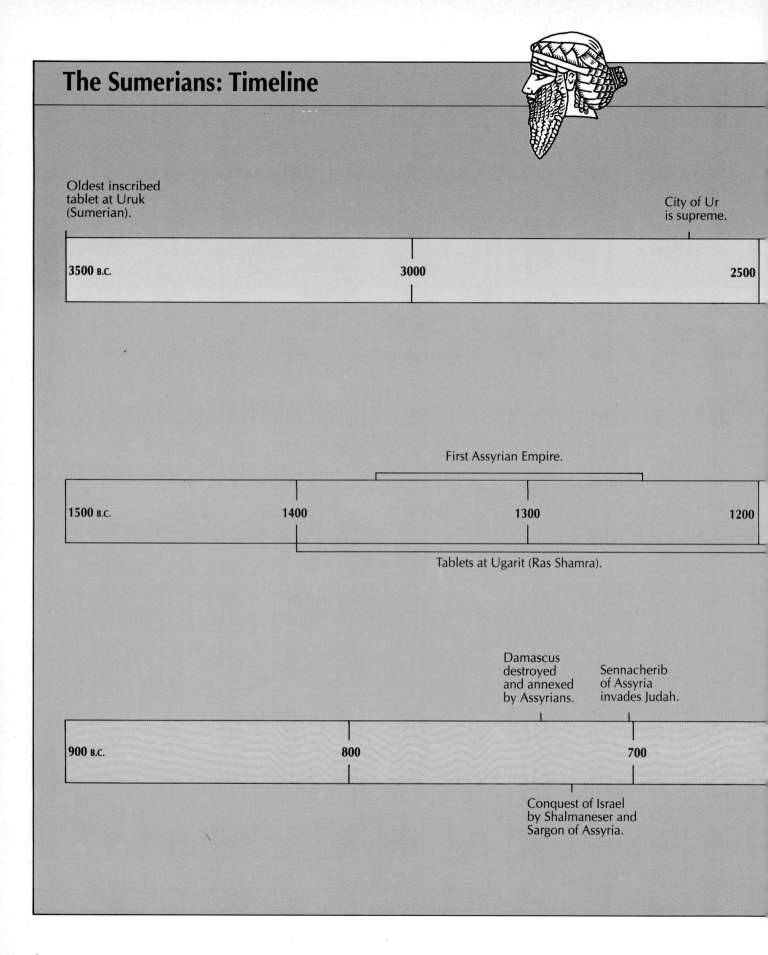

Oldest inscribed tablet at Uruk (Sumerian).

City of Ur is supreme.

3500 B.C.	3000	2500

First Assyrian Empire.

1500 B.C.	1400	1300	1200

Tablets at Ugarit (Ras Shamra).

Damascus destroyed and annexed by Assyrians.

Sennacherib of Assyria invades Judah.

900 B.C.	800	700

Conquest of Israel by Shalmaneser and Sargon of Assyria.

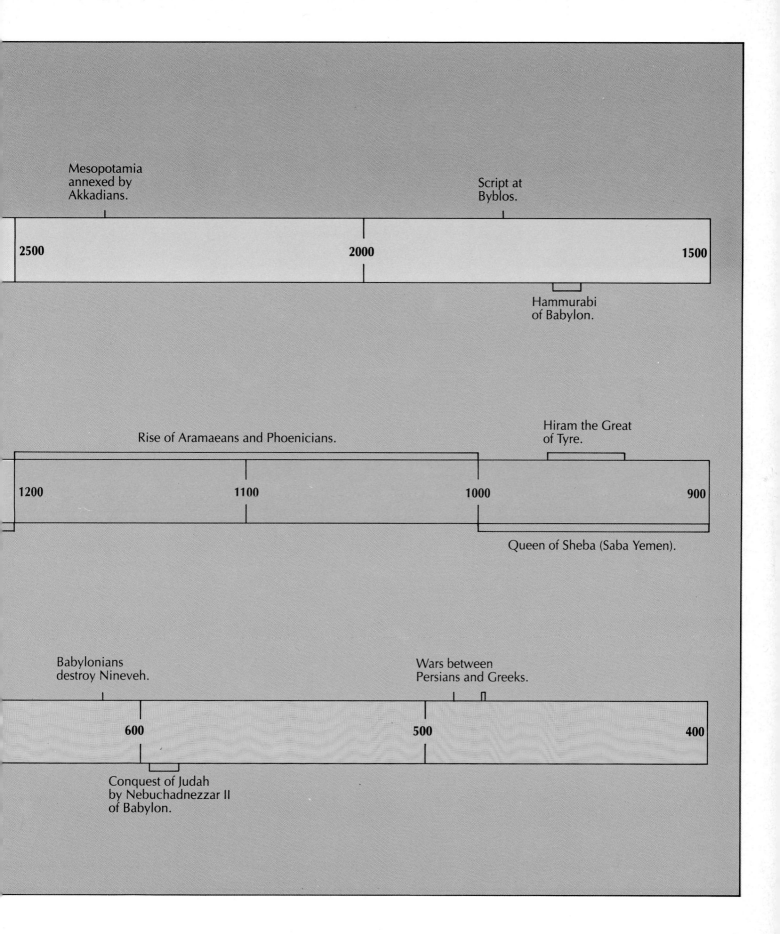

Mesopotamia annexed by Akkadians.

Script at Byblos.

2500   2000   1500

Hammurabi of Babylon.

Hiram the Great of Tyre.

Rise of Aramaeans and Phoenicians.

1200   1100   1000   900

Queen of Sheba (Saba Yemen).

Babylonians destroy Nineveh.

Wars between Persians and Greeks.

600   500   400

Conquest of Judah by Nebuchadnezzar II of Babylon.

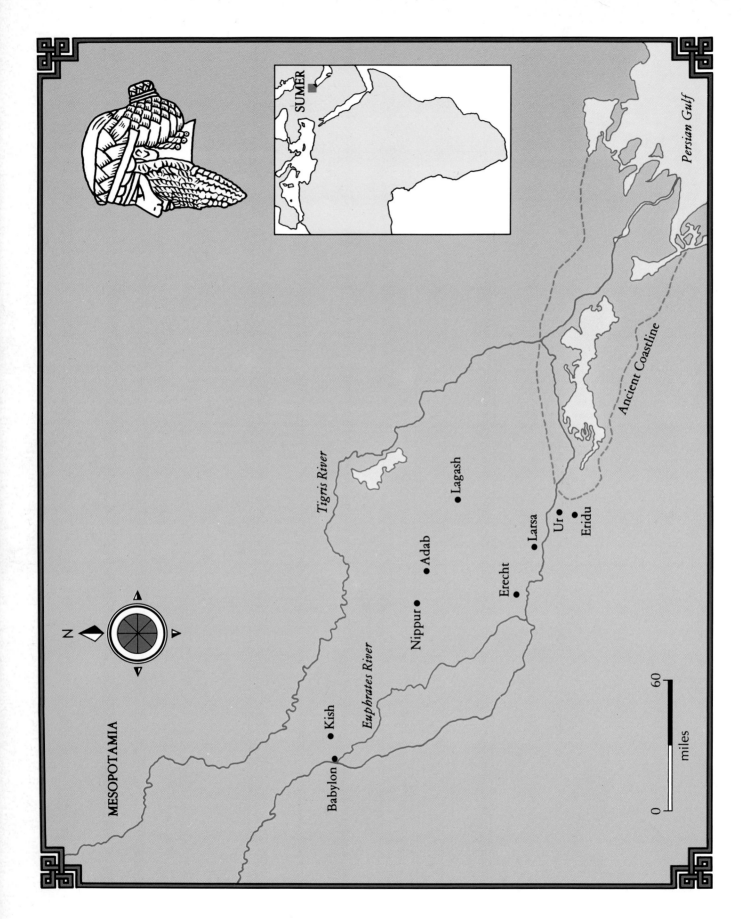

MESOPOTAMIA

SUMER

Persian Gulf

Ancient Coastline

Tigris River

Euphrates River

Babylon

Kish

Nippur

Adab

Lagash

Erecht

Larsa

Ur

Eridu

N

0   60

miles

The Sumerians: Introduction

The Sumerians inhabited the lands of Mesopotamia between the Tigris and Euphrates rivers (modern Iraq) in the beginning of the fourth millennium B.C. Where the Sumerians lived originally or what route they took into Mesopotamia is unknown. But in Mesopotamia the Sumerians established the oldest literate and urban culture in the world. Their earliest cities were Eridu, Ur, Larsa, Isin, Adab, Nippur, and Kish.

Each Sumerian city-state was independent and was ruled by its own king called a **lugal,** or **en,** who presided over a very well controlled and ordered society. Each city had many fine public buildings including temples. Important temples had a huge tower, called a **ziggurat.** The temple was the main center of each city because its high tower rose above the other buildings. Most work, law, and formal education was controlled from the temple. The Sumerian farmlands had efficient irrigation systems of dikes, canals, and reservoirs.

Most Sumerians were farmers, fishermen, merchants, scribes, craftspeople, and homemakers. Rich and powerful families owned large estates (apart from the temple estates), and poorer families also owned houses, farms, and animals. The population could be divided into three classes: free citizens, clients (connected to the temple or to the lands of the estates), and slaves. The Sumerians were very practical people and valued good harvests, healthy animals, family life, justice, and success. There was also a sense of cooperation in their communities.

The Sumerians had personal gods, with each major god owning and dwelling in a temple. The lands surrounding the temple were worked for the god as the Sumerians believed that mankind was created to work and provide for the gods.

Detail of the Standard of Ur showing the king on his throne. Each Sumerian city had its own king.

In 2350 B.C. the Akkadian Empire under Sargon I began in Mesopotamia. The Akkadians were Semites from the north and conquered many city-states of Sumer. After 300 years the Sumerians regained control of their lands and the Sumerian king took the title of "king of Sumer and Akkad." The period of prosperity that followed ended in about 2024 B.C. when another tribe of Semites, the Amonites, invaded from the north. Their later king, Hammurabi, King of Babylon, became king of all Mesopotamia (including Sumer), which became part of the vast Babylonian Empire.

Less than a century and a half ago scholars did not know that the Sumerians had ever existed. When archaeologists began **excavating** in Mesopotamia, they were searching for the remains of the Akkadian culture. But during their search they also discovered remains of the Sumerian culture. The key to deciphering the Sumerian writings lay in first being able to decipher the Semitic Akkadian writings, which in earlier days were referred to as Assyrian or Babylonian.

The Standard of Ur (Peace Side) enables us to know a little about how the ancient Sumerians lived.

The Importance of Landforms and Climate

The Sumerians settled in the south of Mesopotamia, which was known as the land "between the rivers." The two rivers were the Euphrates, which was 1,720 miles (2,760 kilometers) long, and the Tigris. The Tigris was 1,250 miles (2,000 kilometers) long. Sumer occupied the lands close to the Persian Gulf.

The Euphrates was a long, winding, and slow-moving river with few **tributaries.** The riverbed was unstable and floods easily

changed the course of the river. The Tigris was a more swiftly flowing river with many tributaries, but the floods were more severe than those of the Euphrates. In ancient times both these rivers flowed separately to the sea. The rivers constantly flooded, covering much of the area of Sumer with **silt**. The floods started each year when the snow melted in the Caucasus Mountains in the north where both rivers began. As the **water table** of the area has risen over the centuries, remains of the Sumerian civilization have become buried underwater.

The silt carried by the floodwaters kept the farmlands fertile so crops could be grown all year around. This fertile land was bounded by the rivers and surrounded by barren desert. The land had no minerals and practically no stone.

Sumer had a hot climate with only a little rain, less than 8 inches (200 millimeters), in the winter months. The summers were hot and dry with average temperatures being about 94°F (34°C).

The Sumerians adapted to these conditions and used them to their own advantage, producing crops by using irrigation, and keeping animals that were suited to the environment.

The city of Ur, in Mesopotamia.

Natural Plants, Animals, and Birds

Because of the harsh, dry conditions, very few natural plants grew in Sumer. From swamps in the south, the Sumerians gathered reeds and tied them into bundles to be used as building materials or plaited them into mats. These mats were often plastered with mud and used to build huts in very early times. Date palms grew, but the wood of these was only suitable for rough beams.

Other natural vegetation had to be able to withstand droughts. Low bushes and shrubs, grasslands, and some vines grew. Thorn bushes grew in the driest areas, while a few small clumps of trees, including poplar, willow, licorice, and tamarisk, grew by the more permanent water reservoirs.

With little vegetation there was not a great deal of natural wildlife; but gazelle, ostriches, wild asses, and lions roamed the land. These animals are no longer found in this area. Smaller animals included bats, rats, jackals, hyenas, and wildcats. Animals that were

Records show that the ancient Sumerians hunted the gazelle that once roamed the Sumerian lands.

Impression of a cylinder seal showing two ibexes indicates that these animals once lived in Mesopotamia.

domesticated by the Sumerians were not native to the area.

There were many snakes and other reptiles. In early times fish were numerous as texts record over fifty different varieties being found in Sumerian waters.

Crops, Herds, and Hunting

The main crops grown by Sumerian farmers included barley, wheat, and **emmer.** Farming was a carefully planned activity. Archaeologists excavating at Nippur found a farming manual written on clay tablets describing each step, from the preparation of a field to the harvesting of the crop.

Vegetables were also grown in gardens that were protected by specially planted trees, which shielded the vegetables from the heat of the sun and provided a barrier to winds. Gardens were cultivated with a hoe and a special implement called a **garden harrow.**

However, none of these crops could be grown without a regular supply of water all year round. The Sumerians showed a very advanced knowledge of irrigation. They constructed canals, dikes, dams, and reservoirs, which crisscrossed the farmlands. These devices controlled and held the waters of the flood so that there was sufficient water during the dry times. This activity would have involved skills of surveying, mapping, and the use of measuring and leveling instruments.

Detail from the Standard of Ur showing a Sumerian with goats and a cow.

How the Barley Fields Were Managed

1. After floodwaters had subsided and the field was still wet, shod oxen were let loose to trample the fields, level the surface, and kill the weeds.

2. The surface was finally leveled with small, light hoes. Men with pick axes smoothed the hoof marks in the wet mud.

3. While the earth was drying out, the farmer prepared the plow and tools, including whips to be used on the animals. An extra ox was obtained if possible to pull the plow.

4. The field was plowed twice with two different plows, one called the shukin and the other, the bardil plow. Then the field was harrowed and raked three times. Clods of earth were broken up with hammers.

5. The final plowing and sowing of seed was done simultaneously with a special plow fitted with a seeder. The seed was dropped into the furrow and was planted at intervals of "two fingers." (One "finger" was an ancient Sumerian measure equal to approximately $\frac{1}{2}$ an inch, or 1.6 centimeters.

6. When the first shoot appeared, the farmer said prayers to Ninkilim, the goddess of field mice and vermin, so the crop would be protected.

Seal impression showing cult figures celebrating harvest and crops.

7. Shoots were watered for the first time when they filled the furrow; for the second time when the "straw stood high as a mat in the middle of a boat"; and for the third time at "royal barley," meaning when the shoots had reached full height.

Harvesting

1. Harvesting was done before the ears of barley had bent over from their own weight.

2. Three men worked as a team: a reaper who cut the crop with a clay **sickle,** a binder who bound the barley into manageable sheaves or bundles, and a stacker who put the sheaves in piles.

Threshing and Winnowing

1. The mounds of barley were trampled by driving animal-drawn wagons over the crop.

2. A threshing sled, made of wood with teeth fitted with leather and kept in place with **bitumen,** was then drawn over the field to "open the barley," meaning to allow the grain to separate from the straw.

3. Men then separated the good grain from the chaff as it was loaded with shovels.

   Domesticated animals that were kept by the Sumerians included oxen used for pulling plows and carts; bulls; cows; sheep for wool; goats for milk, meat, and hides; and pigs for fat, skin, and meat. Horses were to be found in Sumer in later times but were not used much. The earliest known domesticated pigs were recorded as being at the village of Jarmo in 6750 B.C.

Hunting

The records show that people hunted deer, wild boar, and gazelle, and that fowlers netted birds. Fish were caught in large quantities by fishermen using nets, traps, and lines. We are also told that **mastiffs** were used to hunt lions.

How Families Lived

Sumerians lived in walled cities surrounded by villages and hamlets out in the farmlands. Sumerian houses were made from clay or mud brick. Most houses were one story high, and built as several rooms grouped together around an open courtyard. More wealthy people built two-story houses with the ground floor having a reception area, kitchen, lavatory, servants' and slaves' quarters, and probably a private chapel. Some tenements had three stories. House walls were whitewashed.

Reed mats were placed on the floor, and wall hangings hung on the walls.

Large and small houses were built together in a haphazard way along narrow, winding streets and alleys. Water was drawn from wells and a system of drains took waste from the towns.

Furniture

Furniture consisted of low tables and high-backed chairs. Wooden-framed beds were also used. Baskets and chests were used for storage and as ornaments. Furniture made of bronze and ivory has been found in royal tombs in the ancient city of Ur.

Men

Men were considered the head of the family. Men worked either as craftsmen, as temple personnel, as personnel on estates owned by the temple or wealthy citizens, or on their own farms. Most were farmers, boatmen, fishermen, or merchants. The better educated were scribes, teachers, architects, and doctors. If a man was a client of the temple, he worked for the temple or its lands, and if he was a client of a wealthy man's estate, he worked for that estate. Craftsmen included sculptors, potters, jewelers, carpenters, leather-workers, **fullers,** and metalworkers.

Women

Women were concerned with the important job of caring for children and teaching them the values of the Sumerian culture. Mothers and fathers had equal authority over their children. Women were not always given the same formal education as men; but women scribes do appear in the records. Women did participate in industry and commerce as they frequently ran their own business. They also worked in the textile industry, spinning and weaving cloth of wool and flax. Most families had slaves to help with the household chores.

Children

Children had to obey their parents, who could disown them or sell them into slavery. Education was available for children of the upper classes. Scribes taught reading, writing, religion, law, and medicine, which prepared students to become scribes, copyists, librarians, and teachers. When children were old enough to marry, their marriages were arranged by their parents.

Children could also be adopted.

The Sumerian School

The Sumerian school was called the **edubba,** meaning "tablet house," and was at first the place where scribes were taught to become recorders and administrators. Later, these schools came to include lessons in botany, zoology, geography, mathematics, astronomy, and language. Here, also, books and stories of the past were copied and new ones written.

Sumerian houses were made of clay and mud brick.

Only children of the wealthy, who had money to pay for lessons and time, attended the school. Peasants and others had to work all day.

The head teacher was called the **ummia.** There were also teachers in charge of each subject. However, very little is known about how lessons were taught.

Slaves

Prisoners of war from other countries or from other Sumerian city-states became slaves. Children were also sold into slavery, and free adults could be made slaves by the courts as punishment. Slaves worked for whoever owned them. They were usually well-treated because healthy slaves could work harder. The average price for an adult slave in the market was 20 shekels of silver, often less than the price of a donkey.

Slaves did have spare time and could work for others during their own time to earn money to buy their freedom.

Food and Medicine

Food

Barley was the main food crop, which was used to make cereal cakes and beer. Other grain crops, such as wheat, were also ground to make flour, which was made into breads and cakes. Date palms were grown and a sweet honey called **lal** was obtained from the dates.

Vegetable gardens were grown in the shade of trees. Vegetables grown included **chickpeas,** lentils, **vetches,** onions, garlic, lettuce, turnips, cress, leeks, mustard, and cucumbers.

Food was cooked in clay vessels and pots over a fire and served on clay or metal dishes. Stone, copper, and bronze were used to make utensils.

The Sumerians' favorite drink was beer, which was made from barley. Ninkasi was the goddess of beer preparation and had at least one hymn of praise written to her. Milk was also a popular drink.

Medicine

A Sumerian doctor was called an **a-zu.** Many Akkadian medical texts exist that include Sumerian words, but only two Sumerian medical texts have been found. These texts contain the oldest medical prescriptions known in the world. They have been difficult to translate because terms used are not properly understood today and also because parts of the clay tablets have been damaged. Most seem to refer to the making of **poultices** from parts of plants crushed with oil. Others refer to medicines, which were made from beer, river bitumen, oil, salt, ashes, wool, milk, turtle shells, water snakes, and plants such as thyme, mustard, and the wood of willow, fir, and pine trees.

Many times the Sumerians also included special prayers, spells, or incantations in their medical cures.

We do not know what diseases or conditions the Sumerians suffered from apart from accidents.

Veterinarians

The Sumerians had people to care for the health of animals. There are references to the "doctor of the oxen" and the "doctor of the donkeys," but very little is known about these veterinarians.

A replica of a Sumerian frieze shows workers milking a cow and pouring the milk into butter churns.

Clothes

Stone relief of the Amorite god Baal.

Sumerian temple sculptures and carvings give us the best idea of how the Sumerians dressed. Their clothes were made of finely woven wool and linen.

Men

Men draped their garments around the lower part of the body and tied them at the waist, leaving the upper part of the body bare. Some sculpture shows men in long tiered skirts. In later times the men also draped garments over the upper part of the body to the neck.

Men wore their hair long and parted in the middle. Some wore beards and others were clean shaven.

Women

Women wore a flounced skirt in early times, which was later replaced by a long straight skirt. A large fringed shawl worn over the skirt was draped over the left shoulder, leaving the right arm bare. Long shawls covering the body from head to foot were also worn.

Hair was usually plaited into one plait, which was wound around the head; and women had headdresses of ribbons, beads, and pins.

Wealthier men and women wore soft leather shoes while sandals were worn by everyone else. Jewelry consisting of bracelets, necklaces, anklets, rings, and earrings were worn by Sumerian women.

Opposite: man and woman embracing.

Religion and Rituals of the Sumerians

Sumerian View of the Universe

The universe was heaven and earth to which the Sumerians gave the name an-ki. The earth was thought of as a flat disk with a hollow space above it and enclosed with a lid. Between heaven and earth was lil, meaning wind. The universe was believed to be controlled by superhuman and immortal beings whom people had to obey and serve.

A large number of gods or deities were worshiped with prayers and sacrifices. People were instructed to pray to their god in times of misfortune, and it was believed that the god would turn the misfortune into good fortune.

Next Most Important God
Nanna
The moon god, also known as Nanna Sin. His son was the sun god, Utu, and his daughter was the goddess Inanna (also known as Ishtar).

Sumerian statue from the Kingdom of Lagash, 2150 B.C.

Four Most Important Sumerian Gods and Goddesses

An	The heaven god and responsible for the calendar and seasons.
Enlil	The storm god, known as the "father of the gods" and "king of heaven and earth"; he brought the rains and prosperity and fashioned the first agricultural tools. Ninlil was his wife.
Enki	The water god and god of wisdom who organized the earth as directed by Enlil.
Ninhursag	The earth goddess and the great mother-goddess, called "the exalted lady," goddess of stony ground and its wildlife, goddess of birth.

Other Gods and Goddesses	
Nanshe	A Lagashite goddess who ruled over moral conduct.
Nidaba	Goddess of writing and accounts.
Ereshkigal	Goddess of death and gloom.
Dumuzi	The herder god, god of fertility.
Ninurta	God of the stormy south wind.
Ishkur	The rain god.

Ziggurat at Ur (restored).

There are many myths and legends about the gods and goddesses.

After Death

The Sumerians believed in a life after death. Excavations of royal tombs at Ur and elsewhere have shown that everything a king might require in an afterlife was buried with him. Sacrifices of oxen and sheep were also made for the important dead. The Sumerians believed, as did many others in the ancient world, that the dead would be ferried across a river by a boatman on their way to the other world. To the Sumerians, this other world was sometimes described as being above the earth and at other times below it.

Temples

The center of religious activity was the temple where the god dwelt. All temples contained a shrine, which had a place for a statue of the god and a mud brick offering table in front of it. In later times the shrine was enclosed in an inner room.

Temple Personnel

The head of the temple administration was called the **sanga,** and kept order and directed staff. The spiritual head of the temple was called the en. The en, who could be a man or a woman, lived in a special place called the gipar in the temple.

Other priests, called guda, mah, ishib, gala, and nindingir, were in charge of such things as singing and music. Others were involved in religious services (priestesses) and administration (clerks, officials), directing the work of the temple and its lands. Farmers, laborers, and slaves worked on the temple lands.

The destruction of a temple was one of the greatest disasters the Sumerian people could imagine.

Feasts and Festivals

Several main feasts are mentioned, such as the Month of the Eating of the Barley of Ningirsu, the Month of the Eating of the Gazelles, and the Month of the Feast of Shulgi.

There were many regular monthly feasts held at the new moon and on the 7th, 15th, and last day of each month. A special feast and celebration was held at New Year.

Obeying the Law

The Sumerians believed in law and order, justice and mercy, and compassion, and they organized a system of laws around these principles. Laws are usually made by those who govern, and in Sumer, the ruler was a king, called a lugal. To help govern and advise the king was an upper house, or "town meeting," which was probably made up of members of noble families and wealthy merchants. There was also a lower house of assembly, probably composed of the common people. It would seem that the Sumerians had some say in the making of the laws they were expected to obey.

The king was responsible for all law and justice. However, the carrying out of the law was left to the **ensis**. Some records indicate that judges had this power also.

Courts had procedures to be followed: oaths were taken, written documents were presented as evidence, and both parties were given an opportunity to speak. A **mashkim** (similar to a bailiff) was the deputy of the court.

Written Laws

Written laws were very important to the Sumerians. Many laws and records of legal transactions have been found, as well as law codes. They include the Ur-Nammu law code. Ur-Nammu reigned about 2100 B.C. as the founder of the Third Dynasty of Ur. Yet another code of law was the Lipit-Ishtar law code, 150 years later, intended for use both by Sumer and Akkad.

Some Sumerian Laws

Marriage	Marriages were arranged and were recognized by law. Marriage contracts were often inscribed on clay tablets. Women retained rights after marriage such as owning property, having a business, or having the right to testify in court. Divorce was common, and husbands could have more than one wife if the first wife did not have any children. Children could be adopted.
Slaves	Slaves were treated as property, which could be bought and sold. However, slaves also had legal rights and could engage in business, borrow money, and buy their freedom.
Punishments	Punishments were listed as part of the law. One example is: "If a man has mutilated with a weapon the bones of another man...he shall pay one **mina** of silver."

Other laws concerned gifts, sales, the appointment of temple officials, and inheritance, to mention a few. Where there was no clear punishment, the judge or judges would decide punishment. The later Babylonian **Code of Hammurabi** included severe punishments. Hammurabi, the ruler of Babylon, took over southern Mesopotamia in 1760 B.C. He had his laws inscribed on **stelae** and positioned in public places throughout his empire.

Writing It Down: Recording Things

The Sumerian language is the oldest written language in existence. The Sumerians invented a system of writing that enabled people to communicate with one another and to record things of importance. From this, learning was possible. The oldest inscription on stone dates back to 3200 B.C., and already from about 3500 B.C., clay tablets were used in Uruk to record things.

The writing on these clay tablets was done with a wedge-shaped **stylus** and known as **cuneiform writing.** On these clay tablets scribes kept records, drew up contracts and official documents, recorded laws and legal judgments and sales. Eventually other things were recorded such as formulas, procedures, legends, prayers, and hymns. By 2700 B.C. libraries were established in Sumer. At Tello an archive of 30,000 clay tablets was found.

In 1846, Henry Creswicke Rawlinson became the first person to decipher Mesopotamian cuneiform writing.

Ebla tablet-list of Sumerian professions.

Recording Time

Calendar

The Sumerians had two seasons:

emesh	which means summer;
enten	which means winter.

Months were lunar months and began with the evening of the new moon. Each month was either twenty-nine or thirty days in length. Names of the months varied from city to city and were often names of local feasts or events. A special month was inserted periodically to adjust the calendar to the solar year.

Hours

Days began at sunrise and lasted twelve hours. Nights also had twelve hours and were divided into three watches of four hours each.

Water Clocks

Water clocks were used to measure the hours. A water clock was a vessel with intervals marked on the inside and a small hole in the bottom. The vessel was filled with water and time measured by the intervals above the water line.

Sumerian clay tablet with cuneiform writing. Receipt for a large number of bronze and copper tools, checked by weighing. Dated from 2050 B.C.

Weights and Measures

The Sumerians had their own system of measurement, as shown here. Translations of Sumerian words are given when known.

Measures of Length

𒋗𒋛	šu-si		"finger"
𒆬	kùš	= 30 su-si	"cubit"
𒄀	gi	= 6 kùš	"reed"
𒎏𒁰	nindar	= 2 gi	
𒂠	èš	= 10 gar-(du)	"line"
𒁕𒈾	danna	= 1800 gar-(du)	"league"

One kùš is about 20 inches or 50 centimeters.

Measures of Area

𒊬	sar	nindar^2	"garden"
𒄿𒆪	iku	= 100 sar	"field"
𒁓	bùr	= 18 iku	
𒊬	šár	= 1080 iku	

One sar corresponds to 376 square feet or 35 square meters.

Measures of Capacity

𒄀𒅔	gín	
𒋝	sila₃	= 60 gin
𒄥	gur	= 144 sila
𒄥𒈗	gur-lugal	= 300 sila
𒄥	gur₇	= 3600 sila

One sila₂ equals 0.850 liter (almost one-fifth of a gallon).

Measures of Weight

𒊺	še		"grain"	
𒄀𒅔	gín	= 180 še	"shekel"	One ma-na corresponds to about 500 grams
𒈠𒈾	ma-na	= 60 gín	"mina"	
𒄀𒌑	gú	= 60 ma-na	"talent"	(approximately 1 pound).

Numbers

The Sumerians had two number systems: one for everyday use and one for mathematical texts. Their system was sexagesimal, that is, it was based on the number sixty. The Sumerians did not know about the concept of zero.

Fractions

Value	$\frac{1}{3}$	$\frac{1}{2}$	$\frac{2}{3}$	1	2	3	4	5	10	60	600	3600	36,000
Old													
New													

Mathematics

Texts of tables and problems have been found that contain calculations and formulas such as those used to calculate areas. Although these tables are Akkadian, the technical terms used in them are Sumerian, so they must be based on Sumerian knowledge of mathematics.

600 sag nindar × 600 sá = 1080 × 3 + 180 × 2	= 3600 iku
(60 × 9)(60 × 9) = 1080 × 2 + 180 × 4 + 18 × 2	= 2916 iku
(60 × 8)(60 × 8) = 1080 × 2 + 180 × 8	= 2304 iku
(60 × 7)(60 × 7) = 1080 + 180 × 3 + 18 × 8	= 1764 iku
(60 × 6)(60 × 6) = 1080 + 180 + 18 × 2	= 1269 iku
(60 × 5)(60 × 5) = 180 × 5	= 900 iku
(60 × 4(60 × 4) = 180 × 3 + 18 × 2	= 576 iku
(60 × 3)(60 × 3) = 180 + 18 × 8	= 324 iku
(60 × 2)(60 × 2) = 18 × 8	= 144 iku
etc.	

Sumerian Legends

The Sumerians first began to record their legends in writing in about 2500 B.C. Before this time many of their legends were passed on by word of mouth.

Legends of the Kings

The first ruler of Sumer was a king called Etana of Kish whose name appears on a king list. A legend and a legendary poem describe his ascent into heaven to find a special plant called "the plant of birth." Etana was assisted by an eagle which he rescued from a serpent's pit. His ascent into heaven is illustrated on many Sumerian seals.

Other kings believed to have a connection with the gods were King Meskiaggasher, and his son, Enmerkar. Two epic tales have been written about Enmerkar. Other Sumerian legends discuss Lugalbanda, Enmerkar's herald who became a ruler.

Dumuzi was believed to be both a god and a king. The legend, "Dumuzi's Death," discusses Dumuzi's dream of his own murder by people from the nether world. Dumuzi tried to hide but was betrayed.

Gilgamesh was a hero of many Sumerian myths and legends. Other poems and legends about Gilgamesh and his companion, Enkidu, were written in Akkadian and other languages of western Asia.

Apart from legend, the real deeds and battles of Sumerian kings were also recorded.

One ancient legend told of a great flood sent by Enlil because mankind's noise kept him awake. A pious king was warned by Enki. He built a boat and survived. This legend was passed on to the Babylonians and the Israelites. The legend appears in the Bible as the story of Noah and the Great Flood.

Legends of the Gods

Gods and religion are the subjects of many Sumerian myths. Some of these myths are listed below.

God	Name of Myths
Enlil	"Enlil and Ninlil: the Birth of the Moon-god."
	"The Creation of the Pickax."
Enki	"Enki and the World Order: the Organization of the Earth." (This is the longest of the Sumerian tales).
	"Enki and Ninhursag."
	"Enki and Nimmah: the Creation of Man."
	"Enki and Eridu."
Nanna-Sin	"The Journey of Nanna-Sin to Nippur."
Ninurta	"The Deeds and Exploits of Ninurta."
	"The Return of Ninurta to Nippur."
Dumuzi	"Dumuzi and Enkimdu."
	"Dumuzi's Death."

There are no legends about ordinary people; they are all about gods, goddesses, and kings. Other literature includes love songs, songs to accompany marriage ceremonies, laments for dead gods, and collections of proverbs. A list of some Sumerian proverbs appears on the following page.

Cuneiform writing, which was invented by the Sumerians, was used by many Near Eastern civilizations.

Sumerian Proverbs

"He who eats much can't sleep."

"Tell a lie; then if you tell the truth it will be deemed a lie."

"In an open mouth, a fly enters."

"Friendship lasts a day; kinship lasts forever."

"A scribe whose hand moves as fast as the mouth, that's a scribe for you."

"A cat – for its thoughts! A mongoose – for its deeds!"

"Who possesses much silver may be happy,
Who possesses much barley may be happy,
But he who has nothing at all can sleep!"

Art and Architecture

From earliest times architecture was the main art form. Temples were very ornate with platforms, cellars, columns, facades, and painted walls and altars. Temple statues were skillfully

Below: he-goat nibbling the leaves of a tree found in the great death pit at the Royal Cemetery of Ur. The goat is made from gold, silver, lapis lazuli, shell, and red limestone.

made. Plaques, stelae, vases, and bowls often had carvings on them.

The most notable feature of Sumerian temples was the huge rectangular tower, called a ziggurat. The ziggurat was made of mud bricks with the outer bricks baked and set in bitumen. This tower rose in regular stages and had stairways leading to it. The Nanna Temple of Ur was one of the most important temples.

Interiors of temples were elaborate. The Nanna Temple of Ur, for example, had pale-blue enamel tiles and rare wooden panels of cedar and cypress inlaid with marble, **alabaster, onyx, agate,** and gold.

Cylinder Seals

The Sumerians used cylindrical seals. These cylinders of stone are of particular interest. The stones were carefully engraved with animals, legendary figures, scenes, or other designs. They were then rolled over wet clay to form an imprint.

Copperwork

The excavation of royal tombs at Ur has uncovered detailed copperwork. One of the most outstanding pieces was found on the temple at Al 'Ubaid. It shows an eagle with a lion's head holding two stags in its claws.

Jewelry

Jewelry, made of gold and silver and containing semi-precious stones such as **lapis lazuli, carnelian,** and **topaz,** was considered a work of art.

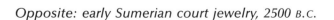

Opposite: early Sumerian court jewelry, 2500 B.C.

Vase from Lagash, third millennium B.C.

Carving and Sculpture

Sumerian sculpture, particularly in later times, shows high technical skill. Figures were carved on stelae, plaques, vases, and bowls. One of the earliest examples of Sumerian sculpture is a limestone face of a life-size statue excavated at Tall al-Warka. This sculpture is now at the Iraq Museum in Baghdad.

Going Places: Transportation, Exploration, and Communication

Materials and goods were transported in animal-drawn sledges, wagons, and chariots, or by pack animals or boat. Wagons had two or four wheels and were drawn by oxen. Smaller chariots were drawn by donkeys and asses. Sumerian boats were of many sizes and were built of precious wood in special shipyards. Boats were drawn along the riverbank by animals or propelled with oars, punting poles, or sails.

The Sumerians did not travel much beyond their lands, although some were traveling merchants who went from city to city and to other lands. When needed, raw materials were obtained from foreign lands either by trade or by force. In these instances conquered people would be taken as prisoners, and transported to Sumer to be forced into slavery.

Sumerian wheels.

Detail from the Standard of Ur (War Side), showing a four-wheeled chariot drawn by donkeys.

34

Music, Dancing, and Recreation

Music and singing were important parts of Sumerian life. Sumer was the first culture to have professional musicians. Both men and women participated as singers and instrumentalists, and some priests had special authority in this area. Music, singing, and dancing were especially important in the temple, although these activities were not confined to the temple. They also took place in homes, palaces, market places, and processions.

Bull ornament from Ur, third millennium B.C.

Silver lyre from Ur, third millennium B.C.

Musical Instruments, Poetry, and Singing

Harps and lyres have been found in royal tombs, as well as drums, tambourines, and pipes made from reeds and metal. Other instruments included the **sistra**, **timbrels**, and drums. Harps were usually played by women.

Poetry and singing were taught in schools and in the home. Many hymns to the gods have been found, including the great Sumerian hymn to Enlil. In writing and performing these hymns, the Sumerians established the foundations for **liturgical music** in world religion.

Wars and Battles

Frequently city-states struggled with one another or were attacked by invading people from time to time. The kings of city-states established regular armies that were equipped with chariots and heavily armed soldiers. Soldiers fought in close formation with shields held high. The armies were well trained and well led, though they only comprised a small

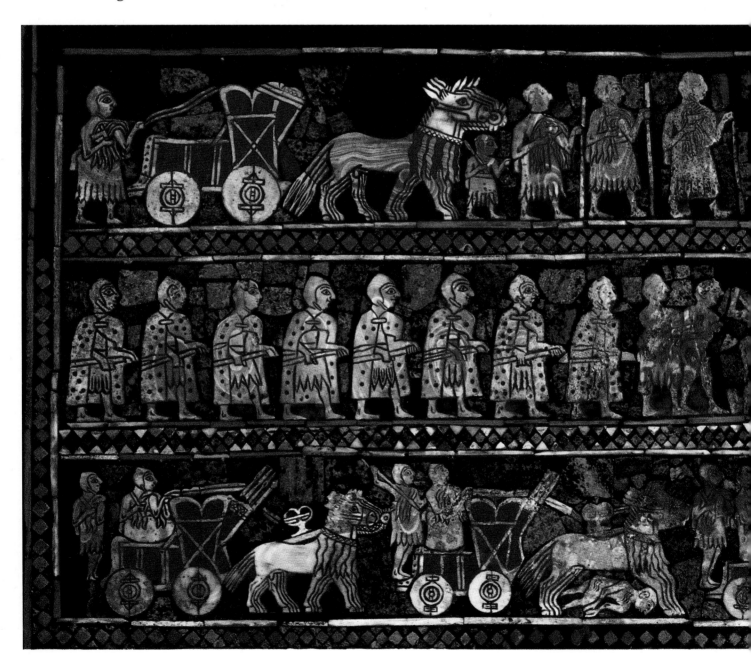

section of the total community.

It is also thought that the army was used to forcefully obtain some of the raw materials needed by the Sumerians, but lacking in their own country.

The Akkadian, Elamite, and Amorite Invasions

In 2350 B.C. the Akkadians invaded Mesopotamia and established the capital at Agade in the north. Under their leader, Sargon I, the Akkadian armies invaded and captured many Sumerian cities extending his rule to the Persian Gulf as well as to the Mediterranean. Sargon's great empire, the first in history, lasted only a short while and the Sumerians eventually regained control of their lost lands.

The Standard of Ur (War Side), showing the Sumerians in battle.

Ceremonial helmet of Sumerian king.

The Amorites and Elamites were people of neighboring lands who made many attacks on cities of Sumer, including Ur. These people were finally driven out and Ishbi-Erra became king of all Sumer. His descendant, Lipit-Ishtar, regained lost lands and took the title of "King of Sumer and Akkad."

Invasion of the Babylonians

The ruler of the northern Semitic city of Babylon was Hammurabi. In 1760 B.C. he conquered all lands between the Tigris and Euphrates rivers. Hammurabi became ruler of the Babylonian Empire, which reached from the Persian Gulf to the Habur River and included Sumer.

Arms and Armor

Copper and bronze were used to make weapons as well as knives and agricultural implements. Lance points, arrow heads, swords, and daggers were made in Sumerian foundries for the armies.

Gold dagger and its sheath were some of the artifacts excavated from a queen's tomb at Ur.

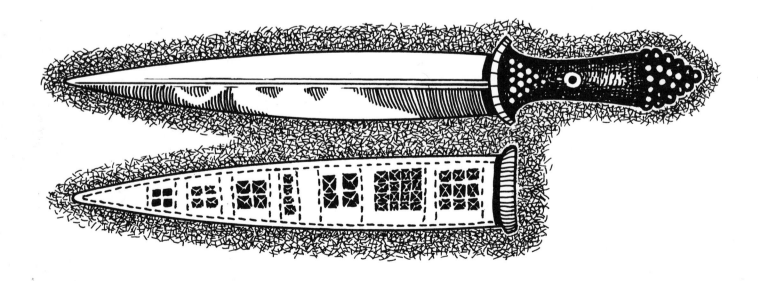

Sumerian Inventions and Special Skills

The Sumerians were the first to invent many things and to devise new systems. The following are some of the most important.

Writing

The invention of Sumerian cuneiform writing was a great achievement. This enabled things of importance to be recorded so people could learn about a variety of things outside their own personal experience.

Written Law

Legal transactions and the rules people in society were expected to obey were among the first things the Sumerians recorded with their new writing. It is thought that the codes of law of other ancient civilizations were based on the Sumerian system of written laws.

Mathematical Notation

Mathematical notation was a great Sumerian contribution to science. It was based on the number sixty. Our system of measuring circles and angles has its foundations in this system.

Wheeled Vehicles

Sumerian inscriptions dating back to 2800 B.C. used a **pictograph** character of a sledge with four wheels. Royal tombs at Kish, Sura, and Ur contained wheeled vehicles. Pictures of wheeled vehicles also appear on works of art and clay models that have been found. The Sumerian wheeled vehicle was probably the first in history. The potter's wheel is also thought to have been a Sumerian invention.

Use of Clay

Sumer had little stone, minerals, or wood, so river clay was used to make most of the things they needed. From clay the Sumerians built their houses and great temples, sickles, pots, plates, and jars. And it was on clay tablets that the Sumerians learned to write their history, literature, and scientific discoveries.

Irrigation

The Sumerians constructed canals, dikes, dams, and reservoirs to hold and later divert precious water to the dry farming areas. Without such irrigation systems, the land would not have been suitable for growing enough food to support the population.

Religious Tradition

Many of the religious traditions and religious myths of the Sumerians were absorbed into the Babylonian culture and passed on indirectly to the Israelites. Sumerian literary works have many themes in common with the Bible, such as the creation of man, the Great Flood, the Tower of Babel (thought to be a Sumerian ziggurat), the organization of the earth, and the concept of a personal god.

Why the Civilization Declined

The Sumerians, who were non-Semitic people, were always under threat from the Semitic people to the north. They were invaded first in 2500 B.C. by the Akkadians (who were Semites); and although the Sumerian rulers of Ur regained control for a period, the Semites invaded again in about 2025 B.C. This time the Semites took over the city of Babylon and in 1800 B.C., their king, Hammurabi, became King of Babylon. Hammurabi conquered all of Mesopotamia and established the Babylonian Empire. Babylon, on the Euphrates River, became the major trading center.

Because Sumer was a collection of city-states, each with its own small army, there was no strong national defense. The Sumerians were not united by a mutual defense system.

The Babylonians then became dominant in culture and civilization, overshadowing the Sumerians. However, many aspects of the Sumerian culture were absorbed into the culture of the Babylonians who, in turn, influenced others such as the civilizations of Crete, Greece, and Rome.

Though the Sumerians were conquered by others, their culture, inventions, and contributions to world civilization and learning continued through its conquerors.

Opposite: statue of a servant of Hammurabi. In 1800 B.C. Hammurabi became king of Babylon and ruler of the lands that were the Sumerians'.

Glossary

A-zu Sumerian name for a doctor.

Agate A semi-precious stone that was a variegated type of quartz. It had colored bands and other markings such as cloudy and mosslike coloring. It was used for ornaments and jewelry.

Alabaster A fine granular gypsum, often white and translucent and used for ornamental work such as figurines.

Bitumen A black tar or asphaltlike substance used in painting and sealing to make things watertight.

Carnelian A semi-precious stone of a reddish color used in making jewelry.

Chickpea A leguminous plant which has pealike seeds that can be eaten.

Code of Hammurabi Law code introduced when Hammurabi of Babylon took over Sumer in 1760 B.C.

Cuneiform Writing A system of writing used in the ancient Near East; the earliest documents in cuneiform were written in Sumerian. The writing was done on soft clay tablets with a wedge-shaped stylus.

Edubba A Sumerian word meaning "tablet house" and used to describe a school, where writing was done on clay tablets.

Emesh Sumerian name for the season of summer.

Emmer A variety of wheat, which was grown in ancient times. It was sometimes fed to animals.

En Sumerian name given to the spiritual leader of a temple.

Ensi A governor or local ruler in the city-states.

Enten Sumerian word for the season of winter.

Excavation A place where earth, mud, and debris have been carefully removed to uncover ruins or remains of a culture from earlier times.

Facade A face or front of a building that is usually ornamented.

Fuller A launderer whose job it was to clean or to thicken cloth to make it compact, like felt.

Garden harrow An agricultural implement with teeth used to level land and break up clods of earth after land has been plowed. It does not have wheels.

Lal A sweet, honeylike substance extracted from dates and used to sweeten food.

Lapis lazuli A semi-precious stone of a deep blue color and consisting of several minerals mixed together and compacted. It was used for ornaments and in making jewelry.

Liturgical music Music used in ceremonies of public worship.

Lugal The Sumerian word for king.

Mashkim A person in the courts whose responsibility was to investigate complaints and follow trials so as to testify about them later if needed.

Mastiff Large, very strong short-haired dog.

Mina A Sumerian unit of weight approximately 500 grams or one pound (1 lb.).

Onyx A semi-precious stone, which is a type of quartz having straight layers or bands that differ in color. It was used for ornaments and in jewelry.

Pictograph A pictorial sign or symbol or a record consisting of picture signs.

Poultice A soft, moist mass or dressing made from various things such as bread or cloth and soaked in a special mixture. It was applied as a medical treatment to part of the body.

Sanga The administrator of a Sumerian temple.

Sickle An agricultural implement with a long curved blade attached to a handle and used for cutting stalks of grain or grass. The oldest Sumerian sickles were made of hard-baked clay.

Silt Fine sand and earth carried by rivers from the uplands, where the rivers run more swiftly, and deposited as a sediment on the lower lying areas.

Sistra Ancient musical instruments like rattles. They were often used in religious ceremonies.

Staele An upright slab, pillar, or sculpture bearing an inscription.

Stylus A pointed stick used for writing on clay tablets.

Timbrel Musical instrument similar to a tambourine.

Topaz A semi-precious stone that has crystals of various colors, including yellow. It was used in ornaments and jewelry.

Tributaries Streams contributing their flow to a large stream or river.

Ummia Sumerian name for a head teacher of a school.

Vetch Leguminous plant grown for its edible seeds. It can also be fed to animals.

Water table A level in the ground where water begins to saturate the earth. It can come closer to the surface or drop away for many reasons. The water table is closer to the surface in low areas, such as river valleys and near the sea.

Ziggurat A huge tower of a temple. It was made of mud bricks and had stairways.

The Sumerians: Some Famous People and Places

UR

Ur was an ancient Sumerian city and is thought to have been the home of the biblical Abraham. Under the Sumerian kings, Ur was the capital of the whole of southern Mesopotamia. Excavations have uncovered royal tombs containing much precious treasure and art, as well as other artifacts. A temple dating back to the first dynasty of Ur has also been found here. The famous ziggurat to the moon god, Nanna, was built here during the Third Dynasty. The last king to build at Ur was Archaemenian Cyrus the Great.

NIPPUR

This was an ancient city where, according to Sumerian mythology, the storm god, Enlil, lived and where the gods met. It is also the place where the Sumerians believed the first people were created.

A great number of Sumerian-inscribed clay tablets have been found here. A ziggurat to Enlil was built here, but was later buried. By A.D. 300, Nippur had fallen into decay, and by the thirteenth century, this city had been completely abandoned.

KING GUDEA

King Gudea lived from about 2144 B.C. to 2124 B.C. and was ruler of the Sumerian city of Lagash. Under his rule Lagash experienced a golden age of arts and learning. He also reconstructed the temple of Eninnu and the temple of the god Ningirsu.

UR-NAMMU

Ur-Nammu ruled Ur from about 2112 B.C. to 2095 B.C. and is best known for writing the Sumerians' oldest law code. His law code dated from about 2100 B.C. and dealt with such things as marriage, divorce, bodily injuries, and the escape of slaves. He also embarked on a massive building program in honor of the chief gods of the city, Nanna and Ningal. He built the great ziggurat at Ur. He also built quays for trade and irrigation works. In Nippur he rebuilt the temples of Enlil and Ninlil and other temples. He also provided upkeep for the temples and installed high priests and priestesses. By about his fourth year in power, Ur-Nammu was accorded the title of King of Sumer and Akkad. He proclaimed for all Sumer the first extensive code of laws in history. He proclaimed his code of laws in the name of the great god Utu.

This body of Sumerian laws was adopted by the Babylonians as a basis for their legal code, which was developed during the reign of Hammurabi from 1792 B.C. to 1750 B.C. This code became known as the Code of Hammurabi.

URUK

Also known as Erech, Uruk was one of the greatest of ancient Sumerian cities and was located northwest of Ur. It was enclosed by large brick walls about 6 miles (10 kilometers) in diameter. An inscription of later date states that these walls were built by Gilgamesh. The two main gods worshiped at Uruk were Anu (An), the sky god, and the goddess Inanna, "Queen of the Sky." The city had many ziggurats. It was a very prosperous city and scribes were still working on ancient cuneiform documents here in 70 B.C.

GIRSU

This was one of the most important cities of ancient Sumer and was located halfway between the Tigris and Euphrates rivers. The city was excavated by French archaeologists between 1877 and 1933, and over 50,000 cuneiform texts were found.

Some of the most important monuments in this city are the Stelae of the Vultures, built to celebrate the victory of King Eannatumm over Umma, and an engraved silver vase of King Entemena. Sargon of Akkad controlled the city from about 2334 B.C. to 2279 B.C. The city was particularly prosperous under King Gudea.

The modern name for Girsu is Telloh. Another important city in that region was Lagash (modern Al-Hiba). Until quite recently it was thought that Telloh was Lagash.

LUGAL-ZAGGISI

Lugal-Zaggisi was a Sumerian ruler who reigned from about 2375 B.C. to 2350 B.C., and who conquered many cities including Kish, Lagash, Ur, and Uruk and united all of Sumer. He then extended his territory to the Mediterranean. After his long reign of twenty-five years, he was defeated by Sargon, the Semitic ruler of Akkad.

ENHEDUANNA

Enheduanna is the earliest known woman poet. She was the daughter of Sargon of Akkad and served as en priestess of the moon god. Nanna in Ur. She wrote a cycle of songs in praise of the most important temples in Sumer and an impassioned poem directed to the goddess Inanna asking for help when a revolution in Ur threatened her life.

ERIDU

This was an ancient Sumerian city located to the south of Ur. The list of kings indicates that this city was the most ancient in Sumer. The god of the city of Eridu was Ea or Enki, "lord of sweet waters that flow under the earth." The city had many buildings and temples, and was occupied until about 600 B.C.

It was excavated between 1946 and 1949 by the Iraq Antiquities Department.

Index